Journey of Two Souls

A Mother and Daughter Story

LINDA DARLENE MARIE SHARPE

Copyright © 2018 by Linda Darlene Marie Sharpe

All rights reserved. This book or any portion thereof may not be reproduced or transmitted in any form or manner, electronic or mechanical, including photocopying, recording, or by any information storage or retrieval system, without the express written permission of the copyright owner except for the use of brief quotations in a book review or other noncommercial uses permitted by copyright law.

Printed in the United States of America

Library of Congress Control Number:		2019932483
ISBN:	Softcover	978-1-64376-128-2
	eBook	978-1-64376-129-9

Republished by: PageTurmer, Press and Media LLC

Publication Date: 06/26/2018
Revised Date: 01/30/2019

To order copies of this book, contact:

PageTurner, Press and Media

601 E., Palomar St., Suite C-478, Chula Vista, CA 91911
Phone: 1-888-447-9651
Fax: 1-619-632-6328
Email: order@pageturner.us
www.pageturner.us

CONTENTS

Foreword ....**viii**
Prologue ....**xi**
Acknowledgement...**xiii**
Introduction ....**xiv**

Chapter 1: She Is My Mother....................................1

Chapter 2: I Am the Daughter 11

Chapter 3: The Change, The Cause.........................17

Chapter 4: Alzheimer's versus Dementia.................21

Chapter 5: The Art of Caregiving 27

Chapter 6: Contending with Challenges 32

Chapter 7: The Role Of Faith and Spirituality.............36

Chapter 8: Grieving 43

Chapter 9: Moving On...49

Bibliography..**53**

To all mothers and daughters
who take on the journey of caregiving.

FOREWORD

It was a cold February morning. I was in a wheelchair as I had fractured my leg. The funeral, in many ways, was a blur. I was the cantor for the service, so I was escorted to the altar by my godson, whose funeral home handled the arrangement. People began to arrive. My sister was surprised at how many had come to celebrate Mother's life. Father Tim was concelebrant with Father Patrick. Music was part of Mom's life. She was a welcoming person, so we began with "Gather Your People, O Lord." Our psalm was the music version of Psalm 23 "Shepherd Me, O God." Our alleluia honored her heritage with "Celtic Alleluia." Mom supported our parish school's STAR program, so we had school children do the general intercessions. Our communion hymn was "Prayer of Saint Francis" as Saint Francis was her patron saint. Mother had a devotion to the Blessed Mother, so for our meditation, I chose "On This Day, O Beautiful Mother."

Whenever we left from home, Mom would bless our travel and pray for a safe journey. So as we send Mother on her journey, we said the "Traveler's Prayer." Because of the winter temperature, Mother's committal took place at the parish. The hymn was "The Song of Farewell"; Mother had a strong faith, so it was only fitting that the sending-off hymn was "Lead Me, Lord." We continued our celebration at the parish hall with a lovely luncheon provided by our Saint Gerard

Guild which Mom was a member of.

This journey that Mother and I have taken is the object of this book.

*Music from Breaking Bread by Oregon Catholic Press, Portland, Oregon

PROLOGUE

As Mother's family, we felt it appropriate that she tell her own story. She is at peace with her Father in heaven. She flies on eagle's wings.

I was born in New London, Iowa, to Hiram and Gertrude Amelia Byers (both deceased). I was the fifth of seven siblings (all deceased); I came from a long family of teachers, ranchers, authors, and scientists. In my young years, I was a surgery nurse at Providence St. Vincent Medical Center. After having children, I became a homemaker.

I married Hugh and was blessed with three children. I married Lawrence (deceased), and we were blessed with a daughter. I have eight grandchildren, eight great-grandchildren, and seven great-great-grandchildren. I have a grand collection of Madonna's as I drew my example from our Blessed Mother; I especially drew to Our Lady of the Seven Sorrows. She and I had similar passions.

I was very active in church in Oregon and California: prayer alert, the mothers' club, PTA, and Stephens Ministry; in civic organizations: blood drive volunteer, room mother, master gardener, canvassed for cancer, heart association, home visitors, Rotary Ann, and Chamber of Commerce while we had our business.

My interests were gardening—thus my patron saint is Saint Francis, church, family, reading, walking, word games, music, and theater. I loved traveling and writing and receiving letters.

As I travel the highway over the rainbow, I pray that our good Lord keeps my family and friends in the palm of his hands.

ACKNOWLEDGMENT

To the Alzheimer's Association with their countless resources that supported me through this journey,

To my faith family who keeps me hopeful and grounded,

To my family of friends and neighbors who helped with my mother's care,

To my mother's caregiver for sharing your gift and for maintaining her dignity,

To my family for their love and support for my mother and for their help with making some of the hard decisions we faced,

To my friends for supporting me during this time,

I am thankful to God for my faith and for giving me and my mother comfort throughout this journey.

INTRODUCTION

My mother went to God two years ago. She had lived in my home for twenty years. Mother had lived on her own for thirteen years after my father had passed. I was in the process of buying a home, and we decided to join together on this new adventure. Mother was independent, and at the time of the merger, she was managing an apartment complex. Our big concern was if she could make this home hers as well as mine. We shed a lot of tears in the process. Our family was not patient with Mother; hurtful things were said. "Maybe I should just die," she said. I told her she needed to take her time, pray for guidance. I saw her fragile and vulnerable at this time. I too prayed that I was making the right decision and for the right reasons.

My thought was we could be roomies! We had been so close throughout my life. Mother was involved in all our lives. She was always concerned for our welfare. Mother was proud of all her children. I saw the move as an opportunity to give back to her for all the sacrifices she made for all of us, her children.

After months of prayer and deliberation, we decided to climb aboard together for this new journey.

So welcome to a journey of two souls. This book is a compilation of memories and experiences of a devout mother and a grateful daughter.

It is my prayer and hope that this book will help other families who are in the situation of caring for a parent. It is not easy for a son or daughter to be a caregiver. Those of us who belong to the "baby boom" generation are facing this situation on an increasing basis.

This book is a reflection on the difference of each vocation. It is a sharing of the difficulties of going from being a mother or father to now being in need of care. How do the relationships change? How do we deal with the change? This is about learning the dynamics of dementia and Alzheimer's, what resources are available to us on this journey, and realizing the benefits of being a caregiver. It is my hope that this book will provide you with knowledge and compassion needed to take on this journey and with the comfort of knowing you are not alone.

I asked myself as you will ask yourselves, "Is caregiving a positive or negative or both?"

From my own experience and others', I share words of comfort along with coping strategies. I share reflections of hope and the ability to move on once the journey is complete.

Life is a journey on our road to eternal life. We all have different journeys. On these journeys, it is hopeful that we learn along the way. The main concept we learn is that none of us are meant to stay in this world. Some journeys are slow, and for others, it is faster. The gift we are given at the end of our journey is peace forever with our Creator.

CHAPTER ONE

She Is My Mother

My mother lived to be one hundred. She was born in Iowa to Grandma and Grandpa Byers. She was the sixth child out of seven. The Byers lived on a farm which was fully sustainable. Mom would talk of the joy in their house. Grandma would make huge feasts of ham and chicken, beef corn, and luscious pies for all the family that came to the farm.

Mother used to speak of the mischief she and her siblings got into. Grandma made all their clothes. Mother was so proud of the new coat she received that Grandma made; it had a velvet collar, and she felt like a princess. Grandma told her not to play in it, but kids being kids, mother and her brother played in the hayloft, and she tripped on a rake and got her coat torn. She was so afraid Grandma would spank her. Instead, Grandma told my mother not to worry; she was just thankful my mother wasn't hurt. Mother had the same characteristic. Instead of yelling or giving spankings, she talked to us; the words we hated to hear were "I am so disappointed in you."

When my mother was five, a new little sister arrived. It was 1918. Grandma was weak and caught the dreaded swine flu. Mother took care of her sister the best a five-year-old could. Mother also tended to Grandma's needs, brought her tea and soup, and wiped her forehead like Veronica wiping the face of Jesus. At a young age, the daughter became a caregiver. Grandma survived the swine flu, but her system was weakened.

Mother attended school in a one-room schoolhouse and loved to go to school to read. She played with her dog Shep and rode her horse. Mother used to tell of the fun she had racing through the fields, dreaming of faraway places. Their home was full of love, laughter, and music. Mother's eldest brother played concert violin when not sitting under the big elm tree. Grandma played piano, Grandpa played fiddle, Mother played violin, and Father played clarinet. I can see where the music came from in my life. Mother was also gifted with a sweet Irish soprano voice. She loved all types of music. She sang in church and loved sing-alongs and musical theater. As a child, I remember mother going about her chores while singing and whistling. She was a happy person.

When Mother was nine years old, Grandma got tuberculosis. She told me Grandma's body became fragile after giving birth and getting the swine flu. Mom took care of her sister and household chores. She was unable to participate in after-school activities. She would take meals to grandma and helped her wash up. When Grandpa was ready to put her in the sanatorium, Grandma passed away. Mother told me that Grandma looked so peaceful. She said in her heart that Grandma was at peace and went to God. The wake was at their house, and Grandma was lying in her bed.

Mother, her brother, and her baby sister were motherless. She said she felt lost and wondered what would happen to them. Grandpa did his best, but he was so distraught over his wife's death. Mother told me that she would wake in the night, and Grandpa was gone. They searched the farm and found him just wandering, lost in thought.

Grandpa just did not know how to raise little girls. Mother stated she was blessed to have a caring teacher who answered and explained questions, as she said, "womanly issues." Grandpa remarried. Mother stated the new wife did not like them. The stepmother would not allow my mother and her siblings to play their instruments. She would not let Grandpa have any pictures of Grandma. I told mother in conversation that the new wife was the epitome of the wicked stepmother. Mother laughed and said she never looked at it that way.

Mother went to live with one of her elder sisters. The sister worked, and Mother studied. They did not always agree. Mother admits she was a little wild. As I saw, she was not perfect. It is funny how kids believe that.

Mother moved back to Grandpa's house. She said she wanted a way out of her situation. The foreman at the apple packing shop was charming. His name was. Mother studied nursing at Good Samaritan College.

It was a diploma course. Mother worked at Providence St. Vincent Medical Center in Portland, Oregon as a surgery nurse. Mother had three children.

Mother stated they lived in a boarding house. She tried not to speak negatively about people, especially the children's father. When I asked specific questions, she stated that he had addiction to alcohol, womanizing, and gambling, so household money went to the addictions versus household needs, such as shoes and clothing. Over time, mother's husband became abusive to her. The final straw is when he attacked her with a knife. She needed to protect the children, so she left. Mother told me many times that the move to leave the relationship was scary and not socially acceptable. I told her she was courageous to walk away from an abusive situation, so the children were not scarred. My half sister told me she remembered the abuse and the lack of home. In the divorce, the court did not strip him of parental rights, and Mother was unaware or had forgotten about this. When the children were approximately nine, seven, and three years old, the children's father went to the school and to the apartment and took them away. Mother's nightmare began. Her comment when I asked her was, "I didn't know where they were for two years." She stated that he did this to hurt her and not out of love for the children. The father did not even stay with the children. He left the children in an orphanage, then with a relative of his. Mother hired a lawyer and a private detective. She also found out that the father lied about his name Hugh and that he had another family back east. Mother said it was a nightmare; she did not know if her children were healthy or dead or alive. We can all identify with her pain. She never lost hope or determination to find them.

The lawyer and detective were successful and found the children with their father's relative. Mother got scared as her daughter was very sick with what she thinks was mononucleosis. The children were sent home with mother and her new husband who would become my father six years later.

Before the children were abducted, Mother had met my father when he was a patient at the hospital she worked at. He helped in the search for mother's children. Mother's church helped her hide the children and made them go by their stepfather's name. Therefore, their father never found them. The children found him about six years before he passed away. Mother married my father and the three children took his name. During the six years, my family moved around a lot. The Great Depression was occurring and then World War II. The moves were always for work or need for living accommodations for the family. I found my father's handwritten résumé and all the reasons for the moves. Mom did not return to work; Larry, my father, felt that the children needed their mother at home. He was nine years older than mother and felt that he should be the breadwinner.

My mother was perplexed that father had little contact with his family, especially his mother. She couldn't understand. She told him how she felt losing her mother. How could he abandon his mother? Dad contacted grandmother, and we visited her in Hollister. I was about two years old. Dad's aunt had an orchard and chicken farm there. I met my great-grandmother from Basel, Switzerland. I have pictures of that. What an adventure. Mother and Grandma became close. In a sense, Mother had a mother again. New relationships were formed. Grandma was one of thirteen children. At the time, all her children lived in California, except one who lived on the homestead in White Sulphur Springs, Montana. Each child in the family had special gifts and talents. There were farmers, tailors and seamstresses, retail business owners, attorneys, doctors, and auditors.

Mother and Father moved several times after I was born: from Sutherlin, Oregon, to Roseburg, Oregon; Burbank, California, to Salinas, California, to Redwood City, California (Bay Area). They moved to Portland after retirement as I had moved to Portland, and much of the family lived here and in Seattle. Mother and I tried to discourage the move as my parents were well established. They argued for two years. Dad threatened to leave, so Mom gave in. They moved to Oregon during winter. Father sent mother ahead to find a place to live in. She was stressed to the maximum. My father packed everything and my brother drove the truck with him. Mother found that a lot of her keepsakes, appliances, and cookware were given away. Another stressor.

Mom found a town house near where I lived. The owner and Dad were two peas in a pod. The owners hired my parents as resident managers. Mom showed the apartments, and Dad did maintenance. For their work, they had reduced rent, and they never got a raise so they have affordable housing. Over time, Mom, Dad, and the owners became the closest of friends.

Once settled into the new surroundings, Dad realized that his grandchildren came around less than when they lived in California. Mom took care of the house, and Dad and the owner kept busy with apartment maintenance. Mom planted her garden, and she walked in the neighborhood. I would join her, and we would have wonderful talks.

I learned so much about life, hope, respect, compassion, tolerance, and justice from my parents, grandparents, and great-aunts and -uncles.

Even though Mom wanted to stay in California, she was glad she came. Dad had several medical issues, and being near me gave her the ability to go to doctor appointments and to do shopping. Mom never drove, and growing up, we only had one car. So I became their means of transportation. After Dad's illness was cured, he became less outgoing and more dependent on me and my mother.

In 1980, my father and mother attended their two granddaughters' weddings, and Dad walked them down the aisle. I did the cake and flowers, and Mom made her family-favorite macaroni salad. Mom and Dad were so happy and proud of "their girls." We had the girls stay with us every summer after their father left them. Their mother was working two jobs, and my parents did not want the girls to be on their own. We would take them on trips, camping, and summer bible school. We would get together with my brother's children when stationed in the Bay Area. Dad would take us to Fourth of July parades while Mother did the canning. The girls were very close to their grandparents. Cheri was quite artistic and made a plaque "On Being a Grandma, On Being a Grandpa." She was eleven and just learning calligraphy. Mom and Dad loved her handcrafted work, and they still have it hanged on the wall of our house.

On Being a Grandma

Be always cuddly, warm, and sweet

Make lots of cookies for us to eat

Be understanding, not too strict

Love the dandelions we have picked

Be gentle and kind and never mean

Take us to places we've never seen

Take all these things

add them together,

Then we come up with you,

The best grandma ever!

On Being a Grandpa

Hold us on your lap when we are small

Pick us up and hug us after a fall

Teach us manners and scold us too

Then take us for ice cream when we're

through

Kiss our wee bee stings, wipe our tears

Give us advice for later years

Now do all of this, and I'll be proud to say

That you are the grandpa

Whom I worship today!

Mother gave her children a sense of worth, belongingness, and love. Ever the caregiver, she knew the emptiness of having no mother while growing up. She wanted her children to feel a mother and father's love.

After the weddings, Mother and I noticed Dad's legs were swollen. He was diagnosed with Bright's disease, a form of nephropathy. The doctors said my father had many years left. Unfortunately, Dad fell into the 15 percent that survived only six months. During the six months, Mother was a twenty-four-hour caregiver. My niece gave my dad a bell to ring if he needed anything as his bedroom was upstairs. Of course, Dad used it constantly. He felt isolated; he was fearful. I too participated in caregiving by watching Dad while Mom had her hair done. I did the shopping. I helped with meals and ate with them. During this period, all Mother and Father's children and grandchildren came to see them. My niece and her mother came with the new great-granddaughter to see my mom, and for my dad, it was love at first sight. She was the only great-grandchild he saw. Time was passing, and Dad was more fragile. Mother was fatigued; she drew on her faith. She and I both prayed for healing but added: If unable to heal him, then call him home. One of Dad's favorite holidays was Christmas. He was tenacious enough to live through the holidays. The boys carried him upstairs to my apartment. He was gray in color, very weak, and his urine was red—showing his kidneys were failing. When we looked at the pictures afterward, we were horrified. He had so much love for us that he fought to stay alive so as not to ruin our holidays. My niece, the eldest grandchild, was uncertain on what to give her grandpa for Christmas. We gave him a jogging suit for his comfort. My niece gave from her heart; she gave a picture of herself when she was three with this poem (which hangs in our hallway):

Grandpa's Girl

When she was three, she was quite a ham, as you can see

With a wide open grin and a towhead mess, carrying a doll to match her dress

Grandpa's house was her favorite place to go, where all her childhood memories would grow,

Of carefree days spent in the sun, swimming, skating, and camping fun

Grandpa's girl is a woman now, but her love is for him somehow

She looks at him, and she is little again, holding his hand

She remembers being Grandpa's girl, his very best friend

Oh, if childhood didn't have to end

But inside her heart, she is sometimes three Still Grandpa's girl, and that girl is me.

Thank you for all my beautiful memories

Cheri Lynn

Mom continued to care for Dad until he died. Once Dad passed, Mom's caregiving came to us, the children. I stayed with her and helped with the arrangements. After the service, she turned the day into a wake in her very Irish way. She had friends and family gather and share stories. We toasted to Dad with his favorite drink: Christian Brothers brandy and coffee. We went and played his favorite sport: bowling. I talked Mom into wearing a T-shirt that my eldest brother gave her for her birthday. It had on the front "Sexy Senior Citizen." Everyone broke out in laughter. This was her way of protecting us from sadness. She reminded us that our faith would see us through this difficult time. She and I prayed to our Blessed Mother to help us and for the Holy Spirit to give us strength and bring us to wholeness again.

Mom had many paperwork and record-keeping to do after the funeral. Since she did not drive, I took her to the Social Security Administration, the Department of Veterans Affairs, doctors, and parish. She also got back to her garden, her work at the apartment. I took her to mass on Sundays. I was waiting for the ball to drop and for her to break. Instead, I saw survival in action that she drew from her past. I asked her how she did it. She stated that she believes in facing a situation by dealing with it then moving on, accepting or adapting to the new life journey. It is not to say mother did not grieve or was always stoic. She cried in private and prayed for guidance many times.

After finishing my bereavement leave, it was back to work. It was hard to return to work and leave her alone, but it had to be. I found myself calling her throughout the day to assure myself she was all right. She finally had to tell me to stop as she couldn't get her work done. I laughed, and that night, she and I talked. Together we set up a list of things I would help her with that she could not do or when driving was needed. Mom independently rode public transportation to her appointments. She enjoyed it as she would meet people or go for tea at the mall. She had tenacity, that is for sure.

So who is my mother? She was blessed with compassion, fortitude, and respect. She had a sense of purpose, a woman of boundless faith in God, and she taught us how we could have the same richness in life as she did. She is the woman who feeds, cuddles, and loves me. The one who gave birth to me. I'm her greatest fan. She is my mother. She loved my father; she was always willing to help her children, grandchildren, great- and great-great-grandchildren. She was my best friend, too; I couldn't replace her with another. When I was a child, she taught me love of God and family and for humankind. She taught me to be a good steward of our land. I am so proud of her and miss her so much.

CHAPTER TWO
I Am the Daughter

Writing about myself is not easy. I always thought it lacked humility and modesty. Then there was the song "I Am Woman". I had friends tell me, "If you do not blow your own horn, no one else will." While working, I learned this lesson when asked to do a self-assessment of my work. Reviews required employers and employees to grade their performance. If you gave an outstanding review, you had to comment why. It could affect your merit raise.

I am in my sixty-seventh year at this writing. I was born in Roseburg, Oregon, in 1948. That makes me a baby boomer. I am the youngest of a combined family totaling six people plus parents. My mother and father were married for six years before I arrived. The closest age to me was eleven years old. The eldest (Dad's son) was twenty-five and his sister was twenty-two. My mother's three were sixteen, fourteen, and eleven. I was the baby of the clan. By the time I was seven years of age, I became the only child. My other siblings were off on their life's journey.

When I was born, my father was forty-five years of age and my mother was thirty-five.

Mother always said I was a happy child who was always smiling. She commented that I could entertain myself. Mother told me that my eldest brother, who was sixteen, used to come to the hospital, straight to the nursery, and just stare at his curly-headed sister. My sister who was fourteen spent time in the chapel praying for a girl. The eleven-year-old was not too happy on being dethroned and to a girl of all things; to top it off, I just missed being born on his birthday.

My first two years of life, I lived in Sutherlin, Oregon. It was a time of discovery, and for my mother, it gave her some new gray hairs. I gave new meaning to "terrible twos." I had my first friend; her name was the same as mine, and we were both two. We had fun playing together with our dolls and our dog named Puddles. I liked to help mother in the kitchen, and I would climb on a chair and then fall off. Mother would hang the laundry in the attic during rainy and wintry weather. One day I got away from her, fell through the ceiling opening, and hit the floor. Mother was a nurse and was concerned, so it was off to the hospital. Fortunately, I didn't have a head injury. It was one of my many trips to the emergency room.

My brother, the eleven-year-old, liked to pull pranks on me. When we had a silver frost and power was off, he locked me in a room where it was dark, and through the small window, you could see all the transformers blow. I was so frightened, and from that point, I feared lightning and have claustrophobia. I guess he thought I would go away if he scared me enough.

Many of my memories up to the age of three were from Mom and Dad's recollections and pictures. I have always been inquisitive, and I remember some of my teachers were not excited about my inquiries. I would question everything; that is how I learned. I also read a lot which allowed my imagination to go wild. I could travel the world through books. My interest in theater came from going to my sister's plays and movies that my sister took me to every Saturday. Even the wrestling matches were high drama. I met a vice presidential candidate when his train came to Roseburg; they were called whistle stops. My dog Puddles was not just a pet but a babysitter, companion, and best friend. I would dress her up in doll clothes and push her in the baby carriage, or have tea on the table my father made me—it was red with chairs—under the willow tree. Puddles was supposed to be spayed, but she had one puppy we named Mitzi, coal black with cocker spaniel features.

Mitzi, unfortunately, was hit by a car and died; that was my first brush with death. All of us grieved the loss. Adults brushed it off by saying it was just a dog. I remember the anger I felt; how could they say that about my friend? Thank God for Puddles. Dad and mom helped me bury our puppy, and I made a cross. We recited the Prayer of Saint Francis, the patron of animals.

When I was five, I was my sister's flower girl at her wedding. My headpiece matched my sister's headpiece. My dress was made of pale pink eyelet with lavender lining. My sister wrapped my hair in rags, and I had beautiful ringlets for the occasion. It was a happy day. My sister was like a princess, and her maids-in-waiting were dressed in pastel gowns. The church was like a castle. The mischief I stirred was because of having to stand by the priest for one and a half hours at the requiem high mass. It was much fun though.

An individual trying to describe and define oneself is not easy, and when does it become pomposity? Recently, I read my star signs. It is the first time the description was correct. I think I am a good communicator, and I have many talents. I like public speaking, acting, and singing. I am friendly, much like my mother, and have been called a social butterfly. Once I get the feel of a situation, I can be a jokester. While taking care of Mom and her lapse of presence, I used humor to calm the situation. I am very versatile and resourceful. I did a lot of improvising during mother's illness. I had to adapt to whatever place she was at and react like the characters she brought forth.

At first, this was not easy as I kept trying to bring her back to the present. Big mistake. It just made her more frustrated and angry. I would cry and call my sister. After a while, I talked to the support group, and they advised me to go where she goes.

I do have a quick wit, and I have poise and can fit into any social climate. I attended midshipman's ball; the mayor of San Francisco sent me the invitation. In school, I was head of various organizations including student council. I won scholarships from music educators and art organizations. I was Bank of America woman of the year while in junior college. I knew my father wanted me to attend college, but since my parents were not financially wealthy, I became very resourceful in getting scholarships. I know the sacrifice they made to keep me in Catholic school. I first wanted to be a teacher as I loved all the nuns who taught me, but then there was a glut of teachers and few job openings. My father was a builder, so I decided to be an interior designer; after all, I was a seamstress. I was able to design the model homes in Foster City. It was fun, and it stretched my creative talents, but something was lacking. I finally realized why I was selling myself short. One sister in high school told me that I wasn't college material, although I was in a college prep school and was getting good grades. She said I would do better in the convent than in college. In my charitable, sarcastic behavior, I reminded her that their order was a teaching order, and you needed college to be a teacher. Whatever vocation was there, it was lost.

My goal at that point was to prove her wrong. I started off with dental assisting and received an associate of arts degree. I was on the dean's list. I worked for a while but got disenchanted because of poor wages for the responsibilities I had. So I returned to junior college and got an AA degree in music and performing arts. I wanted to work on Broadway. Always a dreamer. My father suggested that I get a career that pays better so that I could be independent. I turned to science and decided on premed. When I transferred to university and continued my studies, I ran into a roadblock. I couldn't get into a medical school. Then medical schools were not going to invest in women because they believed women would just get married and leave the practice. I took the courses I had taken and changed to medical nutrition. I received a bachelor's degree in dietetics. My first time away from home was my internship in Salt Lake City. It was an adventure as I was the only Catholic in my internship. I took part in many discussions. I became a religious warrior. The cathedral down the street was my haven and I quickly got involved in the music ministry. I always enjoyed the Mormon Tabernacle Choir, so I thought, why not try out? I succeeded in the auditions; I was excited. There was only one obstacle keeping me from getting accepted: I wasn't a member of their religion.

I have always been adventurous and curious. I also get bored easily, so I needed an extraordinary amount of intellectual stimulation, thus my love of reading and classes in a variety of issues. I am diverse in my philosophy. My grandfather and my mother taught me to look for the good in everyone, share what you have with others, and be true to your faith. My philosophical base was the Sermon on the Mount from scripture. That and watching my mother's example of caring for others are the reasons why I wanted to be in a caregiving career. I consider myself successful in my career. When I retired, the number of people who came was diverse: ministers, nurses, doctors, housekeepers, social workers, and administrators. My message to them all was not to allow anyone to diminish their work; for God gave us all gifts and talents, and everyone has a purpose.

Gemini are considered adventurous. My first adventure was to get my books and my dog and go to school. I was three years old and didn't understand why I couldn't go to school like my siblings. My only problem was that I didn't tell Mom I was going. The principal brought me home, and Mom had a few gray hairs from the ordeal. I had a vivid imagination and would design adventure stories with other neighbor kids. Our escapades, such as going down Dead Man's Hill on my bike or doing tricks on roller skates, landed me in the emergency room more times than not. I wanted to do and try everything. I was into swimming, skiing, hiking, golfing, choreograph for synchronized swimming, acting, musical theatre, horseback riding, volunteering for Habitat for Humanity, and implementing fund-raising events. Because I find everything fascinating, it is hard for me to focus on any one adventure or skill and become proficient. I love life, and my imagination is like a sponge; I want to soak up whatever life has to offer. If you want adventure, I am your companion!

Retirement, caregiving, and aging is its own adventure. When my eldest brother's physical health started to decline, I spent much time in Seattle to help him and his wife as she did not drive. Mother came as well. I was still working, so my leaves became more frequent and was threatening my job. Mother, as well, was having difficulty with wet macular degeneration, so her vision was beginning to fail. I took on her finances and her correspondence. My brother died on September 30, 2009. Our family was with him, and we had one sibling who couldn't come, so we had him on conference call. I sang "May The Choirs of Angels". We prayed with him and his family. Mother, like the Virgin Mary, held her son close until he passed on. Mother was never the same after that. Her journey and my responsibilities changed.

CHAPTER THREE

The Change, The Cause

At first, the changes in Mother were subtle. She was sad, grieving, and unnerved that she had no place to visit her son. She dwelt on the question asked to her by my brother's wife: "Don't you think you have lived long enough?" Mother began to lose her spark. I stepped into the realm of caregiver. I was still working, so to juggle caregiving and work was at times overwhelming. Mother loved to garden, but with diminishing eyesight, she fell several times, so we had to do it together. She began to lose interest as her sight worsened. She loved to go for walks. She would go for two-mile walks. She would meet the neighbors and talk about gardening and many other favorite topics. As her vision diminished, we started taking walks together. It was a good time for us to share and talk about the good times. She kept talking about my brother and could not understand why there was no service or military burial. I talked with my sister and my other brother, on what they thought about getting a little marker for Tom, our eldest brother, next to the family plot. We had it placed. We told our sister-in-law and she was livid. We said it was for mother's mental well-being. Mother began to have hallucinations that the person in Seattle was coming after her to harm her. She could describe these individuals down to what they were wearing. I kept trying to bring her back to reality but found that that made her angry. I would open doors and show her no one was there. She did not believe it. She was so fearful, I finally moved her bed into my room. She would often come into my bed because of her fear. She began telling me this was not her house. I would take her around the neighborhood and over to her old house, and nothing was familiar until we got to our house, and she said it was hers. I cannot tell you how many times we did this. Curtains went from open and bright to closed, making the house dark. I was beginning to feel the pangs of isolation.

Mother always kept our house clean. She tried, but her delirium was breaking her down. I finally made an appointment with our brain institute. I needed to know the cause of her predicament. After the exam, we were able to rule out Alzheimer's. The doctor felt the cause was twofold: age-related dementia and delirium from loss of vision.

I started to investigate the cause and look for ways to help us on this journey we were on. Mother was ninety-eight years old when we started our journey. I retired early as Mother's needs were increasing. I tried to organize our lives, but that was futile as the situation was always fluid. I wasn't able to be proactive—just reactive. I found myself getting frustrated. I found myself getting argumentative. This was not me. I would have meltdowns and call my sister and cry on her shoulder. She would get on the phone with mother and try to calm her and reassure her. What I needed was family to help; it did not come. My brother in Nyssa had health issues and could not help. My sister would come occasionally as she could. Her husband had health issues as well. I started to look for support outside the family. I went to the Department of Aging to get a list of resources. Mother could dress herself and do her personal care. I needed someone to be with her so I could run errands, do the shopping, and go to meetings. Mother's short-term memory was being affected, but her long-term memory stayed intact. I found a support group to attend. Their suggestion was to go to the place she was at the time, instead of trying to bring her to the present.

Mother started to divide me into two people: the good daughter and the bad daughter. I would drive her to an appointment, and she would tell me we were going the wrong direction. I would ask her what direction she remembers, and I would follow it. The direction she gave was the same way we were going. Driving home, she told me the woman who drove her was awful and took her the wrong way. I politely told her I would speak to the other woman. I was losing not only my mother, but my pal and companion. She started to call my sister by my aunt's name which really upset her.

We continued at home, but she began to wander, looking for her house. I would catch her before she got out and suggest that we go together. She always came back to our place. I found deception to explain why her furniture was in my house and when and why she moved: I had mysterious people moving when we were not home. Mom still had enough wits about her to know we were not truthful. That deception breaks down trust. I tried to keep her engaged by taking her to dinner with friends or taking drives. As time went on, she would ask me to take her home, she would say that her husband (my dad) needed her, and she could not stay any longer. I would ask her which home, and she would say where Dad was at. She knew that Dad had passed away, but at the same time, she said he was here, and he would get angry if she doesn't get home. It was at that point I knew what she wanted. I told her that anytime she was ready, I would encourage her to go home. In April of 2012, Mom went into a memory care unit. I hated doing this as she didn't understand why she had to go to "jail." She kept asking what she had done wrong. I would spend every day with her and have one meal with her. When I would leave, she cried. When I got outside the locked door, I would cry. It hurt my soul. It felt like I went back on the promise I made to my dad, which was to care for her and keep her at home. We fixed mom's room with her furniture. Friends and family came by to visit. We couldn't go to my great niece's bridal shower, so they brought it to her. We had a great time. We attended all the activities the facility had to offer, trying to keep her engaged. I would sing to her, which I also did at home. In August, my great niece got married, and we took mother and a caregiver as we stayed all night. We had her dancing, and she held her great-great-grandson. Wonderful memories. Mom began to fall more, which meant trips to the emergency room. Her face looked like she had gone twelve rounds in a boxing ring. The staff asked me not to spend so much time at the facility as it was hard on mother, and they weren't able to work with her. I had to put trust in a system I didn't trust.

I was asked by the social worker if I was an only child; I explained our family dynamics. S/he asked if the other siblings were available; I stated not all. One brother had passed, the other was not in good health, and his wife was his caregiver. My sister came when she could but had obligations of her own. So I became "that" child. Mother lived with me. I took her to appointments, and when her vision began failing, I took care of her finances. The social worker stated that my situation is not uncommon. There was always one child in every family. She stated it is often out of sight, out of mind for others.

Friends and associates often said that my mother and I were too tied to the hip and that I had no life. I was indignant at the remark. As always, I try to reflect on the subject. It was my father who kept me cloistered and followed me where I would go. Mom argued with him all the time. Mom especially argued for moving out of state. It nearly caused a split. Eventually, she gave in, and they moved here to Oregon and found a place near me. My father's experience with his late wife taking the children and hiding them made him overprotective.

As a family, we had a strong relationship and it worked for us. I felt God put me here for a purpose, and at this time, it was to be a caregiver. I have never regretted doing it. I just wished I had more tools, understanding, and resources to have kept my mother at home.

CHAPTER FOUR

Alzheimer's versus Dementia

When Mother and I started our journey, the biggest question I had was "What are we dealing with?" Did she have a minor stroke or small vessel disease or depression? My eldest brother had died and all the drama around that, so I took her to the doctor and he felt she had age-related dementia. Mother also knew something was wrong, and when the doctor said she had dementia, she got angry and said she wasn't crazy. She felt as though the medical field was brushing her off because of her age.

I talked to a neurologist I knew, and he suggested the physician at the brain institute. It wasn't easy getting in, but when we did, I inquired what testing could be done to determine my mother's problem. The physician ruled out stroke. He could see some small vessel disease. He ruled out Alzheimer's, there were no amyloids or tangles, no Parkinson's disease. I took her to the ophthalmologist, and he stated that her wet macular degeneration was worse and impairing her vision, and this could cause delirium. I started to research the difference between dementia and Alzheimer's.

I went to the Alzheimer's Association, and they had a wealth of information. Dementia is a general term for memory loss and other mental disabilities that interfere with daily life. It is caused by physical changes in the brain. There are many types of dementia: Alzheimer's, vascular dementia, dementia with Lewy bodies, mixed dementia, Parkinson's, and many more.

Alzheimer's is the most common of the dementias. It accounts for 60 to 80 percent of dementia cases. Alzheimer's is not a normal part of aging, although the majority of cases are people over sixty-five years of age; early onset can occur in individuals in their forties and fifties. One in three people over eighty-five years old has the disease. Alzheimer's worsens over time; it is a progressive disease like Parkinson's. Survival is from four to twenty years and, presently, has no cure.

People with memory loss often do not realize they have a problem; it is more recognized by family and friends. Besides memory issues, Mom became suspicious of family, caregivers, and our intentions. She had sleeping issues at times, woke up fearful and felt she was being followed.

I asked the neurologist what the risk factors for dementia and Alzheimer's are. He told me family history—the disease can run in families because of genetics or environment or both. One myth that has been dispelled is that aluminum is a cause. Research has failed to confirm the role of aluminum.

There are genes involved with Alzheimer's; risk genes increase the likelihood of developing the disease and deterministic genes, which directly cause the disease.

When I look at Mother's family, I could not see any indications for familial Alzheimer's. Mother was never genetically tested, but she did not have amyloids or tangles which associated with the disease.

As I reported earlier, there is no cure for Alzheimer's disease. Medications at this time do not cure or stop the progression of Alzheimer's or dementia; they may only help lessen the symptoms, such as memory loss and confusion, for a limited time. Medications for moderate stages are from a class of drugs called cholinesterase inhibitors. These drugs are to treat memory, thinking, language, judgement, and other thought processes. For moderate to severe stages, the type of medication is Namenda, which is approved by the Food and Drug Administration, for improving memory, judgement, reason, attention, language and ability to perform simple tasks.

Tomorrow's treatments are brought about with clinical trials. TrialMatch service is a free tool to help caregivers and physicians locate clinical trials based on personal criteria and location.

Physicians sometimes prescribe Vitamin E to treat cognitive Alzheimer's symptoms. Do not take Vitamin E without supervision of your physician. Vitamin E is an antioxidant and may protect brain cells from certain kinds of chemical wear and tear. Studies have shown that high doses of Vitamin E in mild to moderate Alzheimer's had a 19 percent slower rate of functional decline. Functional decline includes daily activities, such as shopping, preparing meals, bathing, eating, planning, and traveling.

No one should take high doses of Vitamin E as it can negatively interact with other antioxidants and medications, including those which keep blood from clotting or to lower cholesterol.

Treatment for Behavioral Changes

In early stages of dementia and Alzheimer's disease, patients may experience behavioral and personality changes, such as irritability, anxiety, and depression. In later stages of dementia or Alzheimer's, new symptoms may occur, such as anger, agitation, aggression, emotional distress, physical or verbal outbursts, restlessness with pacing, shredding paper or tissues, hallucinations, delusions, and sleep disturbances.

Situations, such as changes in the person's surroundings, may play a role in triggering behavioral symptoms. We saw our mother have misperceived threats and increased irritability when a new caregiver came, and she became angry and felt imprisoned when we placed her in the memory care unit because the door was locked. Mother was in her late nineties, and for her, using medication was iffy as she had so many drug interactions and allergic responses. My suggestion for elderly people is that there should be a gerontologist who can manage medications and can discuss the risks and benefits.

There are non-medication approaches to treat behavioral changes that should be tried first. Non-drug treatments include recognizing the person isn't just mean or ornery but is having symptoms of the disease; identifying the cause and how symptoms may relate to the disorder; and changing the environment to resolve challenges and obstacles to comfort, security, and ease of mind. When mother was upset, I would ask her what caused it. Mother would say she must have been a bad mother, and that is why we sent her to jail. I would tell her how precious she was to us, and we placed her in the care unit for her protection and security. I told her that the people she felt would harm her would not find her in the facility. Sometimes it worked; sometimes it didn't. When she was angry with her situation, we would go for walks outside for fresh air and conversation.

What I learned through the process is to monitor her comfort, not to be confrontational. In the beginning, I would try to correct her and bring her to the present—well, I became the wicked one. When she insisted that Dad was with us, I even took her to the grave site. Her answer to me is "I know he is dead, but he is here." I realized then that she was seeing Dad, and he was telling her to come home, and he needed her. At that point, I changed my strategy. I tried to redirect her attention if appropriate. We all tried to give her a calm environment. When Mother had sufficient rest, she had fewer behavioral issues. The biggest issue for our family was to not take the behaviors personally. What is hard to cope with is the loss of the relationship we had with Mother and her not knowing us.

Alzheimer's and dementia patients often have sleep disorders or changes in their sleep habits. Scientists do not know why this happens. Older individuals without dementia notice change in their sleep patterns as well. Researchers from the National Institutes of Health (NIH) have found that patients with dementia wake up more often and stay awake longer during the night. Brain studies have shown changes in the dreaming and non-dreaming sleep. Individuals may be drowsy during the day; they can become restless and even agitated (sundowning). This often takes place in the latter stages of Alzheimer's and dementia folks. As a caregiver, this can take its toll on one's own health. Mother had sundowners, and it was difficult to keep her on a wake-sleep routine. She would lie there talking or delirious or pacing around the house. Moving her bed into my bedroom did not help. Non-drug strategies should be tried first. Some of the causes for sleep disorders are depression and restless leg syndrome, which mother complained of as cramps and tingling in her calves. Sleep apnea is another cause. The NIH states that sleep medications do not work on most older folks, can increase chances of falls and fractures, and do not improve the sleep quality. (Alzheimer's Association, Web MD)

Non-drug treatments aim to ameliorate the sleep routine. To create an inviting sleep environment and promote rest, we used the following:

- We put mother on a meal and sleep schedule.
- We made sure she had sun exposure as much as she can in the northwest.
- We had no trouble with exercise as mom enjoyed walking and gardening.
- We avoided alcohol as she did not like it, except for a glass of wine on special occasions. She never smoked, and she had two cups of coffee only in the morning. Remaining beverages were decaffeinated or herbal.

- We tried to limit narcotic pain medication as she did not like them, so we only tried extra strength Tylenol.
- We made sure her bedroom was at a comfortable temperature. She slept warm, so we kept the temperature at around sixty-eight degrees.
- We had night lights in all areas of her travels, bath, kitchen, living room, and bedroom.
- If mom woke up in the night, I would get her up, and we would go for a walk in the house. She usually woke because of delirium. We would talk and reassure her she was safe.[1]
- Instead of television, we played music from her era that she enjoyed. If we used television, it was to watch old movies or documentaries from her era.

If your physician is proposing medication, ask them the benefits and risks of the medication and alternative treatments that are available. Do try the non-medication method first. I also suggest a good geriatrician.

There are alternative treatments, but many do not have scientific research. It is important that they are safe, so look for the United States Pharmacopeia (UPS) label on any supplement. The FDA has to approve drugs but not supplements as they are considered food. Purity is often unknown. Supplements can have serious interactions with prescribed medication. An example is Gingko biloba taken with prescribed blood thinner; it interferes with the drug, increasing the chance of intracranial bleed.[2]

The Alzheimer's Association has a great website with information on Alzheimer's, dementia, and its treatments. The American Medical Association is studying the omega-3 use on dementia, the Alzheimer's Disease Cooperative Study, and the Memory Improvement With Docosahexaenoic Acid Study.

Treatment and care for our loved ones are in constant flux. Stay tuned!

---

1   http://www.caring.com/article/mid-moderate-dementia
2   Physicians' Desk Reference/Pharmacopia

CHAPTER FIVE
The Art of Caregiving

Caregiving is one of the greatest gifts we can give a loved one. It can also be the most demanding. As caregivers, learn to prioritize your own wellness.

Devoting yourself to the unpaid care of an elderly, chronically ill, or disabled family member can make you isolated, exhausted, and overwhelmed. Because I did not recognize this, I saw friends slip away, my work suffered, as did my health—both physical and mental. My faith is what kept me going. When I finally found help, a lot of damage has already been done. Family stepped in and made it clear that I could not continue. I fought it and found a home care company to help me with mother, but Mother and I could not afford the full-time care.

What is caregiving?[3] It is the act of providing help and support to those who cannot care for themselves and their daily needs. Caregiving can entail many tasks, such as giving medication, cleaning, cooking,

---

3   http://www.aplaceformom/senior-care-resources/articles

shopping, paying bills, and helping with activities of daily living. As a caregiver, you are also the provider of emotional support.

Not everyone has the propensity for caregiving, and admitting it to oneself will save a lot of emotional drama for the patient and the family.

Stress can easily creep up on you that being frazzled and overwhelmed becomes normal. You may not realize how much it's affecting you and taking its toll on your mind, body, and behavior. I will cover more on this subject in the next chapter.

With dementia patients where there can be subtle to abrupt changes, it is important for the caregiver to provide a safe environment. My mother lived with me for many years before the dementia set in. We have a one- level home; she knew every aspect of the house. At times though, she would say, "This is not my house." Again, what I was not realizing was that she was actually speaking of her heavenly home.

In caring for my mother, I learned a lot about the art of caregiving. One needs compassion, a positive attitude, patience, and love. I found that keeping a routine is a way to achieve positive caregiving and to decrease the effects of memory loss. Same meal times, same chair, and same bowl. I initiated activities like simple chores, art, and talking to keep her involved in everyday life. Mom had taken care of the house and garden, so we weeded and planted together, and she would pick the flowers. She made her bed and dusted, but we hired out for the big jobs.

Mom would question where we were and why and what should we be doing; she asked to old friends who they were. She was clingy, almost childlike. It is hard, but do not get annoyed. We are now their guide through this confusing world they are in. I tried to focus on her emotion: sad, worried, scared. I tried to orient her if we were going to the hairdresser or the doctor, or if we were already there.

When inappropriate behavior happens, try not to be embarrassed; just smile apologetically and leave. This situation happened at a church concert, and she got scared and made it clear that she wanted to leave. I asked her if she did not want to hear the Christmas music; she said yes, but not there. Looking back, I feel the large crowd and close contact scared her.[4]

As Mom became more aware of memory loss, there were plenty of misunderstandings. She would blame me if things didn't go well. Even mild-tempered fuses go off, and insults, pouting, and threats come to the surface. I was constantly trying to reassure mom that I loved her, but at times, that didn't work, and she would lash out verbally. I wanted to cry because I felt helpless. Every night, I prayed for understanding and patience. My faith and my love for mom kept me going. I never treated or talked to her like a child. I kept smiling, I didn't hurry her, and above all, I had a deep respect for her. One calming method I used was to sing hymns to her, or we would cuddle together and pray the rosary. It brought her peace.

Dementia makes dressing, bathing, toiling, or getting in the car harder as the brain and body are not communicating. She wore clothes that were easier to get into. I prompted her on her grooming, instead of doing it myself. We outfitted her bathroom with bars and a bench so she could still bathe. I helped with hard-to-reach areas and assisted her with getting out of the tub. We never had an incontinence issue when she went into memory care. She wore protection at night, just in case she didn't wake up to go to the toilet. When we went out, I would ask her if she needed to use the bathroom. At home, she would just go to the bathroom on her own.

As a caregiver, I learned about taking a stress check the hard way. When I got frustrated, I would call my sister and vent, but later realized that it would have been better with a friend. My sister lived two hours away, and at times lost patience with both of us. She did not mean to be hurtful. She probably felt helpless and sad for mom's situation. My

---

4 http://www.nextstepincare.org/caregiver_Home/?

brothers would call, joke with her, and make her laugh.

I found myself more and more isolated and should have made time to go for lunch and coffee with friends. The one activity I kept was my small faith group; it was gratifying and grounded me into my spiritual life. I kept my doctor appointments and often took Mom with me. When I couldn't bring her, I had the caregiver come and stay with her and feed her lunch.

As time went on, I found that I was more sluggish and sleep-deprived as my mother would wake in the night, breaking the sleep pattern. At times, she slept with me if she couldn't go back to sleep. Sometimes, our dog would crawl in bed with her and gave her comfort. My health was beginning to go downhill. At the time of my retirement, I was having fatigue, aching joints, and insomnia. As a family, we saw that it was time to look at other living situations. I fought it because I had promised my father to take care of her as she had cared for so many. When we found a facility near me, I was overcome with guilt. Every time they shut and locked the door, I broke out in tears. She would cry, "What did I do wrong to be put in jail?" I prayed and talked to clergy friends to be assured that I made the right decision. I rallied friends and clergy to visit her. I was there every day and had lunch or dinner with her, just so she didn't feel abandoned. The staff asked me to stop as it was harder for them to care for her. It was so hard to stay away.

Once the decision was made to take mom to a memory center, and she was put on hospice, I asked for a geriatric evaluation. The team had medical, nursing, social service, and chaplain. They really managed her care and were with us until the end. The physician guided her medication so she stayed alert and functional. Mom had trouble with falls so the nurse cared for her wounds. The social worker helped me and my feelings over the situation and reassured me that I made the right decision.

At times, mom would get angry and frustrated and would ask why she was in jail. I tried to avoid phrases like "Don't be that way." Most of the time, I just held her, prayed for guidance, and reminded her how much I loved her and wanted her safe.

I finally called the Alzheimer's Association, and they gave me a support group to attend at the local senior center. I found it helpful and eye-opening to say the least. My problems were minimal compared to others. It gave me an outlet; it gave me a community. One of the great-grandchildren was getting married. We couldn't go to the tea so my niece brought it to mom. We had a lovely time. She was able to go to the wedding and be a part of the celebration. I had the caregiver come along and take her to the hotel if she got tired. Mom loved a party, and she stayed to the end. She even danced with the bride and groom. She was able to see all the great-great-grandchildren; a memory we all cherish. My prayer everyday was to have the grace I needed to give mother tenderness and love. I asked the Holy Spirit to give me fortitude and perseverance that mother would never feel she was a burden; instead, she is a gift. Thanksgiving to trinity the courage to answer the call for the healing ministry

CHAPTER SIX

Contending with Challenges

The demands of caregiving can be overwhelming. If you feel you have no control or you are in over your head, and the stress goes unchecked, it can take a toll on your health, relationships, and state of mind. This leads to burnout. Once you reach burnout, it is tough to do anything, let alone take care of someone. To nurture others, you must nurture yourself. It isn't a luxury; it's a necessity. You need to maintain balance.

Even though caregiving is rewarding, it does have stresses. In many cases, including my own, you are dealing with a long-term challenge. There is change in the family dynamics, household and work disruptions, financial pressure, and increased workload.

When your health is at risk, it affects your ability to provide care.

Once my health started to suffer and I experienced isolation from not being with family and friends, it felt like the walls were closing in. My coping skills started to languish.

These are some common signs of stress:

- Anxiety, irritability
- Tiredness or feeling rundown
- Trouble sleeping
- Overreacting
- New or worsening health problems
- Trouble concentrating
- Feeling resentful
- Drinking, smoking, or eating more
- Neglecting responsibilities
- Cutting back on leisure time

I was not so good at noticing that I was burning out. I felt that I had taken on the responsibility, therefore I had to do it alone. I thought I had a good support system. I had people come to visit Mom but no one to stay with her that would allow me downtime. I didn't want to be a burden to them.

So my first recommendation is to ask for help! Speak up, and tell your friends and family that you need help; they do not know your needs.

When I asked for help, a friend and her husband did my groceries when they did theirs. My niece, who is a bookkeeper, took over my finances. When I had an appointment, other friends would stay with my mother. As hard as it is, you have to relinquish control. Mom couldn't do much around the house, so I finally got a home health aide to help with mom's care.

My next suggestion is to take a break. Give yourself time to rest. One of my girl friends came back from east, and she took me to lunch and Saturday market. She gave me an outlet to vent all that was held inside me. It was enough to refuel my spirit. I learned to set aside thirty minutes a day for myself. Often, it was while mom took a nap. I would do yoga or read or listen to music. Find ways to pamper yourself. A sister I knew was a massage therapist, so once a month, she would give me a massage. She would come to the house and give mother a chair massage which made her feel good.

Laughter is the best medicine. I had friends who would have us for dinner and the whole evening was filled with jokes and stories. I felt good, and it was pleasing to see Mom smile.

It is important to stay connected. Go for coffee or lunch with friends and share your feelings. I was worried about burdening them with my troubles, but they were flattered that I trusted them with my inner thoughts. I got to know them at a different level.

I always thought that my folks would live forever, and we would be free of troubles. Unfortunately, life throws us curves. When I think of mother's situation, I would find myself getting angry or confused.

The why question came up. Going down the rabbit hole and trying to make sense of the situation didn't make me feel better. I wanted to blame someone or felt sorry for myself. I prayed for guidance and help to see us through our situation. Once I turned to God, I was able to accept the situation. My mantra became "Let Go, Let God." Mother would say that what doesn't kill us makes us stronger. She was right. We need to focus on the things in our control. One needs to choose how to react to the problem. Try to find a silver lining. How has caregiving made you stronger or a better person? For me, I realized what was important in life. I redefined success. I always felt that my parents did not owe me anything, but for me, taking care of my parents was my way of giving back for all the sacrifices they made on my behalf. I just wanted to share the love. Sharing your feelings can be very cathartic. If you cannot get past the problem, then speak to a therapist or join a support group. Avoiding tunnel vision is important. Caregiving cannot consume your whole life. I put more time into church and ministries. I started swimming; I got back to decorating. So I would suggest finding a hobby or more family time or any activity you enjoy.

Caregiving can take a toll on one's health. Think of your body as a car: If you maintain it, it will run well; if it is neglected, it will give you trouble. It is important to maintain your health. Keep your doctor visits. If you don't maintain your well-being, you will not be able to care for your loved one. I am not a big fan of exercise, but it helps in maintaining your strength. I chose walking since I have a dog that needed it, and I started water aerobics. Exercise is a great mood enhancer and energy booster. I enjoy yoga and meditation; they help calm the body and bring you to mindfulness. I would also do centering prayer or attend a Taize prayer session. Maintaining a healthy diet will give you nutrients to help with stress and sustain your energy for your daily tasks. Mother ate and prepared healthy meals, but when I get stressed. I head for comfort foods which caused me to gain weight and only a quick burst of energy. Mother often woke up at night so sleep was often disrupted, and we were night owls so sleep was less than recommended. As I get older, I need more sleep—at least nine hours. When I have less sleep, I am less productive, I get mood swings, and my coping mechanism suffers. So do not skimp on sleep if you are a caregiver.

I also suggest joining a support group. I found a local one through the Alzheimer's Association. You are meeting with others who are going through a similar situation. You can discuss your problems and listen to others; they help you and you help them. The group knowledge can be invaluable. It was the love from this group that took the sting out of putting mother in a memory care unit.

Besides local support groups, there are online groups. Good for those who cannot leave their homes. I used both local and online. I also utilized my faith-based contacts in decision-making and support.

CHAPTER SEVEN

The Role Of Faith and Spirituality

Spirituality is the aspect of humanity that refers to the way individuals seek and express meaning and purpose, and the way they experience their connectedness to the moment, to self, to others, to nature, and to the significant and sacred. (Nancy Gordon from about health)

The stress of caregiving often causes caregivers to question or deepen their religious or spiritual beliefs. I am not here to tell you how or what to believe. Caregiving needs a holistic approach and that includes spiritual and religious traditions.

Our family is faith-centered, especially mother. Praying the rosary, Sunday Eucharist, prayer team, and doing the altar linens were a great part of her life. She participated in all the Holy Day traditions. I also see church and faith as my spirituality and strength. Science has shown that caregivers who practice their faith have less depression and have better coping skills. Surveys showed that 75 percent of those who prayed on a regular basis to assist them carried out their duties with strength, compassion, good humor, grace, and dignity.

It was important to carry on our traditions. I took mom to Mass on Sunday as long as we could. After mother entered the memory care unit, I would conduct a prayer service for her and was her Eucharistic minister. I had the priest come and give her the sacrament of anointing of the sick. Each night, we said our prayers together, and if I could not be there, we prayed over the phone. I had home visitors come to give her the Eucharist when I could not be there. I wanted to keep her connected to the parish. To get out for exercise, we would walk through the convent grounds of the Grotto and pray the rosary. I facilitated a small faith group; we continued to have mom participate. We brought the group to her at the memory care unit. She was able to connect with her church community.

If you are grounded in a religious background, it is important to stay in touch with the community, its values, and practices that supported you in the past. There were times I didn't feel I could participate in church and the activities because of caregiving duties. Those closest to me, such as the sisters, priests, and church community, reminded me that if I do not receive nurturing, then I will not be able to nurture. Community members came to visit Mom and would take me to lunch. One dear friend did shopping for me. All this love took away the feeling of isolation and loneliness.

My faith allowed me to make tough decisions, especially when it came to priorities in life. It helped me through the emotional roller coaster of caregiving. It is easy to let go of your spiritual practices, but things that are important should be the last and never the first to go. My opinion is they should never be let go.

One can never overestimate the value of a community of persons who share your values and beliefs. Many churches, synagogues, and mosques provide support groups aimed at caregivers.

Caregiving is a selfless act of love, and our spirituality helps us deal with loss. Being a caregiver and being gifted with a deeper connection to our loved one can bring new meaning to our lives.

Spirituality is not predicated upon a certain religious belief. Whether we are priests, deacons, or confirmed atheists, we all have a spiritual side. Express your spirituality and embrace it through the love you show as a caregiver.

There are studies showing that people with Alzheimer's or dementia can benefit from familiar religious traditions, although they do not say how. We were a religious family, and we tried to keep mother involved as best as we could. We loved music, and I used to sing with and to her. She had favorite hymns and songs she enjoyed, so we would sing together. She loved her Irish heritage so Irish hymns and songs were included in our daily get-togethers. We brought mother to St. Patrick's Day festivities at the church, and she reveled in the dancing and singing. Because of the fact that Mother's eyesight was failing, she could no longer enjoy reading. I would read the psalms or scripture passages that brought her comfort.

Another comfort gleamed by mom was Baron, our dog. He was six months old when we got him. He is a Cavalier King Charles Spaniel; my brother bred them and gave me one of the litter. Mom and I made the trip to Eastern Oregon to get him, and it was love at first sight. He sat with her, slept with her, and went for walks together. When she began her journey with poor eyesight and dementia, Baron was a godsend. When my mother felt down, Baron improved her mood through his playful behavior. He had a calming effect on her. Even in her last moments, he laid with her, with his head on her hand, and she was calm and peaceful. Whenever I visited, I brought Baron with me, and the residents lit up with joy.

The *Merck Manual* states that over 90 percent of seniors are religious, and 5 percent find themselves spiritual but not religious. Others identify as atheists who do not seek meaning through religion or spiritual life. In the United States, more than 96 percent believe in God or a higher spirit; more than 90 percent pray; and more than 50 percent attend religious services weekly or more often. Religious participation is greater in the elderly than any other group. To the elderly, the religious community is the largest source of social support and volunteer social activity. It has been found that religion improved physical and mental health. The psychotic benefits of religion are

- a positive, hopeful attitude about life and illness,
- a sense of meaning and purpose in life, and
- a greater ability to cope with illness and disability.

Religious beliefs often foster community which increases the chances of disease being detected earlier. They will most likely follow a plan of care as the community will follow up with the individual. Many churches have a parish nursing ministry that monitor or help members comply with their health needs. Religion, as I mentioned before, helps the caregiver cope with the stresses of caregiving. Caregiving, I found, is a great treasure, a ministry. Care is more than a focus on cure; it carries an opportunity for inner healing and liberation and even transformation. I found this in myself. I considered my work in health care as a caregiver to mother a calling.

> *My true call is to look the suffering of Jesus in the eyes and not be crushed by his pain, but to receive it in my heart and let it bear the fruit of compassion and mercy.*
> —Henri Nouwen, Walk with Jesus

Compassion is not easy; it makes both parties vulnerable. It takes us into the place of weakness, loneliness, and the feeling of brokenness.

As a caregiver and daughter, I wanted to be able to take Mom's suffering and for her to be my pal again and enjoy life; but alas, I couldn't. All

I could do was to be there and not leave her; I would hold on to her and enjoy her as long as I could. By sharing the grief and pain together, that, to me, is compassion.

Caregiving is an ingrained response to suffering. We want to ease our loved one's pain.

Jesus said, "Be compassionate as the Father is compassionate." (Luke 6:36) Before we were caregivers, we are God's beloved children. Compassion is the center of Christian life. When I think of compassion, I think of the Beatitudes, which I feel is a call to compassionate living. I think of Christ on the cross asking the Father to forgive us. There are countless references to compassion in the Scripture.

Telling our story is not only a blessing but a gift to the listener. When we have stories to tell, we have hope. Listening is an active awareness of the coming together of two lives. It is active caregiving. I did not always have this gift. I think now, that God gave my mother's care to bestow this gift. I can see the weaver at work when I listen to people's stories and tell my own stories; our lives meld together, and we become different. "Healing means, first of all, the creation of an empty but friendly space, where those who suffer can tell their stories to someone who can listen with real attention." (From Reaching Out)

During this caregiving and life journey, I had people tell me, "I don't know how you do it (caring for my mother)." In listening to their stories and reasons for not being able to be caregivers, I began to realize the why of their remarks; it is a reluctance coming from our inability to provide a cure for those we care for. To realize that to cry out with those who suffer, to be present in their pain, and to show compassion when they are anxious asks them to face their own pain and fears. In our culture, I see avoidance around the conversation concerning death. When I was in the medical field, I cared for patients in end-of-life care. Besides the patients sharing their vision of death with me, I also became a follower of Elisabeth Kübler-Ross. I took her workshops on death and dying. She was straightforward as she shared her beliefs. It was a liberating experience. I went home and even began a discussion with mom and dad. At first, I think they thought I lost my mind. What I realized is how freeing the conversation was and how our lives and philosophy on life changed.

When we offer care, we can recognize our own pain, fears, and need for healing, and realize our own mortality. We commune with those we care for. Caregiving is about being present for a brother or sister who is feeling powerless. We are not someone who takes the pain away, but we are there to share it.

The responsibility of caregiving can be overwhelming as mentioned in previous chapters. Although it takes time and effort, we need to seek out help. Humble acts of sharing, asking, and receiving allows family, friends, and faith family to realize their own potential for caregiving and saving the primary caregiver from burnout. "Real friends find their inner correspondence where both know the love of God. There spirit speaks to spirit and heart to heart."[5]

I previously said that I considered my work a ministry. This comes from a philosophy that all people needing care are beloved children of God.

I realized that living my faith is to live the Beatitudes and to recognize that human fragility, pain, and suffering won't change that fact. In the Beatitudes, it states, "Blessed are the poor. The people we care for are blessed even though they may not feel this way as they face illness or death." What I realize is that God's blessing is coming to us from those we wish to serve; the blessing is a glimpse of the face of God. Seeing God is what heaven is about; we see the face of Jesus in all who need our care. We have so much blessings; Mom gave me many. I hope to pay those blessings forward. One way that I chose was to write this book of our journey of love and care.

---

[5]   The Inner Voice of Love by Henri Nouwen

As I have said, caregiving is a blessing, but it can be draining. Here are suggestions to maintain spiritual strength:

1. You're Not in This Alone—Seek Support
2. Stay Connected to Your Faith Community
3. Be Open to the Healing Power of Love in Relation to Your Loved One
4. Embrace Acceptance and Forgiveness
5. Remember that You and Your Loved One are Children of the Creator
6. Express Your Feelings Honestly
7. Find Balance Between "Doing" and "Being"
8. Give Up Control
9. Maintain Times of Rest
10. Take Time for Prayer

CHAPTER EIGHT

Grieving

I grieved many times in my life: Death of relatives, death of pets, loss of relationships, loss of innocence, loss of physical well-being, and death of my brothers and my mother—all in a three-year period. After my father's death, my dear mother stated, "Losing someone you love is excruciating. You never get over it; it just becomes less intense." Grief is like being drawn into a mystery. There is no timeline as to how long it will last. The goal is to not get stuck in any other levels of grief.

I have read, "Be patient toward all that is unsolved within you, and try to love the question. The point is to live everything. Do not seek answers that cannot be lived, but love the questions, and perhaps without knowing it, you will live your way into the answers."

What is grief? Grief is not an illness or disease; it is a normal reaction to the death of someone or something you loved. You grieve deeply because you loved deeply. The definition of bereavement is "to be torn apart". When we love those we love. part of our life is torn away. We have emotional wounds, and grief is the healing.

Literature tells us that there are five elements of grieving:

1. Accepting the reality of the loss
2. Experiencing the pain of the loss
3. Recreating the person in your memory
4. Adjusting life without the presence of the person
5. Finding new meaning in life

Each person experiences grief differently. How you grieve depends on your personality. You never forget the person or persons lost. In my case, I lived peacefully with the loss, knowing that mother was at rest and with her family. Grieving changed me that I am more spiritual, and my faith is stronger. I can feel hope in the future.

As I mentioned, everyone is different in how they grieve. There are five stages of grief:

1. Shock
2. Denial
3. Anger
4. Sadness
5. Gradual Acceptance

People sometimes go through the stages in order, some will skip some of the stages, while some experience several at a time. Personally, I never felt anger. When my father died, I was shocked as it was unexpected. With mother and my brothers, it was sadness because they had been ill for some time. In all my losses, I had acceptance because of my faith and faith practices. I was even the cantor at both my father's and mother's funerals. It gave me comfort and strength to give this gift to them and to our family. How a person deals with grief depends on one's personality, family background, how one has coped with past losses, and one's relationship with God.

The big thing is not to let people tell you that your grief is less than others, or that you "need to get over it". There is no timetable for grief. It is cyclical, and emotions have different levels of intensity for months. There were times I felt I had moved on, then something happens and the sadness returns. During the period near Mother's passing, I broke my femur, and so I was dealing with personal loss of independence and anger because I could not be with my mother until the near end. I was angry with myself, and at times angry with God. Why now? I was in a wheelchair when my sister and I spent a four-day vigil with mom. I told her I would be alright, and I knew she was tired, so she can let go of this world. Shortly after that, she smiled with a twinkle in her eye and then passed away. During the vigil, we prayed, and I sang to her. What I felt at that point was that the strife was over. I felt emptiness. My mother, my pal, was gone. I was having therapy for my leg, so I did not have time to feel the loss. Mom had prepared her own liturgy and wrote her own obituary, and I handled the service with her wishes and directions. She had paid for her funeral beforehand, and the plot was purchased when dad died. She took care of us until the end.

Grieving versus Mourning: Grieving is an intense pain one feels inside; it is the internal experience of loss. Mourning is the public expression of grief; it is how we express our sorrow to other people.

I found the death of my mother more devastating than I expected. Mother's death was the end of a life chapter, and the loss of a best friend, a mentor, and a teacher; she lived with me for as long as some people are married. I even had feelings of abandonment. I knew what it was like to be orphaned. I felt empty. I miss her wisdom, her humor, and her reassurance. Mom and Dad kept the family together.

For me, grieving took on physical issues—the stress of my mother's loss and my injury turned into insomnia, increased anxiety, flair of irritable bowel syndrome, headaches, and unwell feelings.

Because of my injury and my mother not being here to help, I felt totally alone. Thank God for neighbors and friends that brought food and helped with transportation.

Having faith helped me a lot. I poured my heart out to God, the Blessed Mother, and Jesus. I offered my pain to Christ on the cross. I prayed a lot.

I never asked why this happened or what caused my mother to die for I knew the answers. I didn't have "what if" moments.

Everyone I met wanted to know what happened, and after a while, I didn't want to talk to anyone, but a priest friend told me that it was part of the healing. He suggested telling the story to a few friends, and after I finished, I could go to the first person and start over. After a while, I didn't need to share anymore. During recovery from my leg injury, I drew upon Mother's strength to get through. I began to feel stronger.

Mother had hospice services during her final days. They had a bereavement group. I decided to go as it was an outlet for telling the story, and confronting my thoughts and dysfunctional feelings. I needed direction. You may wonder how I realized that I needed a bereavement group. I knew my needs, but for others, I offer the following:

- You have no one else to talk to
- You are concerned that your thoughts are not normal
- You are unable to function
- You have thoughts and feelings that you cannot share with anyone else
- You feel like your life is completely out of control
- You feel as if you can't go on

There are many qualified counselors, and you could check with a hospital chaplain, or in my case, a hospice. Catholic services were also helpful.

I had a lot of questions about myself and my response to grief. I had a lot of physical symptoms, such as lethargy, joint and back pain, chest pain, weakness, shaking, hair loss, and insomnia. I finally went to a doctor, and he explained that my symptoms were part of my grieving and also from my arthritis, osteoporosis, my fracture, and my surgery. For grieving, I found a grief support group, and for the physical symptoms, there were exercise, diet, sleep aids (naturopathic), and medication for anxiety. I learned that I had to be patient, especially with myself.

There were times I felt like I was going crazy. I found in my situation that it was because of lack of focus and sleep. I use yoga to help with focus and calming. I focus on the breathing. The following are ideas to work through one's grief:

- Eat balanced meals.
- Avoid alcohol and caffeine; they are depressants.
- Exercise for twenty to thirty minutes a day.
- Lighten your schedule.
- Focus on the present.
- Don't get upset over disturbed sleep patterns. Get up and do something until you get tired again.
- Find ways to release feelings of anger, such as punching a pillow, screaming, or yelling at God.
- Read books on grief.
- Rest three times a day; take time-outs for about ten minutes, and find a mantra that helps, such as "peace" or "help me."
- If you have a prayer life, experiment with different forms of prayer.
- Expect that some days will be worse than others, so be patient with yourself.
- Keep a grief journal.

It has been three years since my mother passed. I visit the grave, and I talk to her and dad. I have vivid memories of our life together.

"God gave us memories so we could have roses in December,"

Ecclesiastes 3:1,4 says, "To everything there is a season under heaven . . . A time to weep and a time to laugh; a time to mourn and a time to dance."

My mother and I had a special bond which will never be broken. Mom has a special place in my heart, but it is time to move on.

CHAPTER NINE

Moving On

What does "moving on" mean? I talked to many individuals who had experienced loss of different types. Loss of job, divorce, death, and loss of health and independence are just a few kinds. All had different concepts for moving on. For the job loss, it is finding new employment or retraining. For divorce, it was to redefine their identity and security for themselves and their family. For me, loss of health and independence was and is finding out my capabilities and limitations, and finding purpose and meaning within my limits. For those who experience death, the first thing they tell me is to never say "move on". My mother's favorite saying after my father died was "You never get over it; you just get used to it."

I read a wonderful article in our local newspaper. The story is about a man who lost his wife of fifty-seven years to Alzheimer's. She is in the mausoleum, and he has visited her over two thousand times in five years or so. He states how much he misses her and that he is still in love with her. The funeral director stated that people handle grief differently; some, like this man, visit daily, while others make pilgrimages. This man talks to his wife and tells her about his day and that someday, they will be angels together. The daily visits let him get to know the staff and workers, and he invites them home during the holidays. He found a new family as he has no children. The visits have given him structure.

A question I ask myself, who am I now? When grieving, that was my identity. After the funeral, my identity became a patient as I was recovering from the fracture that I sustained just before my mother passed away. I was doing physical therapy and healing, and didn't have time for grieving. The grieving began after therapy, and I was alone in the house. I missed our conversations, her smile, and sense of humor. I was lonely because now I was an orphan. I have a half sister, nieces, and nephews, but both of my parents are gone.

What to do about the loneliness, eating alone, making all the decisions, and caring for the house and garden? Abraham Lincoln once wrote, "You cannot now believe that you will feel better. But this is not true. You are sure to be happy again. Knowing this, truly believing it will make you less miserable . . ."

I found comfort from Baron, my dog, especially in the night. I leaned on friends for support. Prayer was very powerful; I tried to imagine Christ's loneliness in the garden. Speaking and listening to Christ was important; I would tell him my feelings and asked him to travel with me on my journey to wholeness.

Grieving can lead a person to temptations; the biggest for me was to look for a surrogate parent. I finally realized that my mother is irreplaceable. Other temptations can be pride when one refuses to admit he needs help, irritability leading to not being nice, complaining leading to criticism of others, doubt when we forget to keep God in the picture, self-pity leading to feeling sorry about ourselves, or despair eroding faith and hope. Prayer is my ammunition against temptation and sharing it with others.

I still get surges of grief but not as much as early on. I tend to focus on all the wonderful memories and happiness my mom and dad gave me.

Scars? Yes, there are scars; I see them as badges of survival. I never felt angry for my loss. I had my mother for sixty-five years of my life, she lived to be a hundred years old, and God granted her a peaceful death.

We can learn from our losses:

- Keep moving because the world doesn't stop for us.
- My troubles are not as important to others. Others may move on quicker.
- Love is boundless. Unconditional love is never lost so follow your dreams.
- Even with loss, one can find peace.
- There is strength in adversity. When I feel self-pity, I focus on those worse off than I am.
- Be grateful for what I have.
- Take control of my life and my emotions.
- Loss is not a reason to give up; I motivated myself to enjoy life, dream big, and set goals.
- I didn't say goodbye, just "See you later, Mom." We will be together again.

I have seen, in my work, daughters and sons who had a lot of guilt at the loss of their mothers. I find guilt loveless. I have seen decisions made that do not reflect what their moms wished but to ease one's own guilt. I was fortunate that our family came together and honored mom's wishes. I, for one, felt no guilt. Our relationship was strong and positive. Yes, she was protective, but she was loyal to her family, offered us encouragement, praised me in my successes, and gave warmth and hugs when we had sadness or what I called failings. As adults, we were best friends. I was fortunate to have my mother with me even through my retirement. I will carry her love and friendship forever. By being the best person I can be, giving back to the world, loving others, being kind and not judgmental, and working for justice for all is the best way I can honor her.

How did I know that my new life has begun? One way was going on a pilgrimage to Ireland, especially after my injury. We celebrated mom in song and a mass said in her honor. It pushed me to not give in; that is how she lived. In other ways, I noticed that my new life was full of laughter, enjoying the world around me, feeling grateful, my eating and sleeping patterns normalized, I have a zest for life and those around me, I feel hopeful, I have found joy in the smallest of things, and I look forward to adventures yet to come. I try to look for ways to improve myself and welcome the new people in my life. I am enjoying all kinds of activities from theater to day trips, lunches, and dinners with friends. I am still working for the poor and disenfranchised through work with the sisters as an associate.

Although my journey with my mother has ended, my journey continues with new memories to forge.

BIBLIOGRAPHY

A Tapestry of Love: The Spirituality of Caregiving : Daphne eRiley and Joseph LaGuardia

    The Spirituality of Caregiving: Henri J. M. Noun

Kimble, Melvin A. and Susan McFadden. *Aging Spirituality and Religion: A Handbook.*

Five ways to get through the first year of loss: Nancy Stout; pamphlet;Care notes;2004

Website:

http://helpguide.org/Harvard/saying goodbye.htm, Coping With a loved Ones Terminal illness.

Saying Goodbye; Barbara Okun PhD, Joseph Nowinski, PhD;Berkley Publishing Group/Penguin Group. 2011

Blog; 9 Things I Learned In the Year After My Mother Passed;Alyssa Sampson; EliteDaily.com/life/live; Nov. 3 2014

When daughters grieve the loss of their mother. Lisa Bonchak Adams; lisabadams.com;5/25/2011

The complete Guide to Caring for Aging Loved One; Tyndale

Press;Focus on the Family,2002

A Shrine To Love and Loss;Beth Makamura;Oregonian/Live;July 30 2016

The Grief Recovery Handbook; The Action Program Moving beyond Death, Divorce and other Including Health Career and Faith; John W. James and Russell Friedman; https://www.griefrecoverymethod.com/ books/grief-recovery-handbook

Melody Causewell; Mother - daughter relationships/Everyday lifeglobalpost.com/typesof motherdaughter-relationships-13135

https://www.griefrecoverymethod.com/blog/6/2013/best-grief-definition-you-will-find

http://psychcentral.com/lib/the -five-stages-of-loss-grief;Julie Axelrod

On Death and Dying; Elizabeth-Kubler-Ross; 1969;McMillan Publisher NY.

Margarit Tartakovsky, MS; On Grief LsOs and Coping; http://psychcentral.com/lib/on-grief-loss-and-coping, jun2e015

Top Ten Spiritual Practices for Caregivers;Rev.Rebecca Ebb-Spies, Director of Pastoral Are;Luther Community; Caregiver resource Network;public service;www.CaregiverResources.net

Family, Religious and depressive symptoms in Caregivers of disabled elderly, Maria Victoria Zunzunegui, Francois eBland, Alicia lLacer, Ingrid Keller:November 1998;Lancet;1999;July

Care Conscious article: Meaning, Purpose and Caregiving:Spirituality and religions Role in Caregiving; hppt://www.careconcious.com

Religion and Spirituality in the Elderly: Merck Manual:Danial Kaplan PhD, MSW;Barbara J. Berkman, DSW, PhD. Merck, Sharp and Dome,

Nj,2016

http://assistedliving.about.com/integratedmedicine/touching-spirits.htm;4/13/16

How Does Pet Therapy Benefit People with Dementia; About Health;.com/do/treatmentsofaltzheimers/a/The -benefits- of -pet-therapy-for- people-with- dementia.htm;4/13/16

Taking Care of yourself;managing stress as caregiver: Alzheimer's Association publication;0408024, CM969Z. www.alz.org,2007.

Caregiver Stress and Burnout: http://www.helpguide.org/articles/stress/caregiving/caregiving-stress-and-burnout.htm.

Caregiving for a Parent or Elderly Person:Patricia St.Clair: Todays Caregiver;http://www.caregiver.com/articles/print/caregiving_for_ parent.htm

Are You Heading for Caregiver Burnout? Paula Spencer Scott; http://www.caring.com/articles/caregiver-burnout-quiz

10 Senior Nutrition Myths; Jeff Anderson; 3/15/14;http://www.aplaceformom.com/blog/3-15-14-senior-nutrition-myths

A Caregivers Guide to Mid Moderate-Stage Dementia;Caring.com Staff; http://www.caring.com/articles/mid-moderate-dementia.htm

Guide to Dementia Care at Home:4/29/2015;http://www.aplaceformom/senior-care-resources/articles/dementia.htm

Alzheimer's Disease and Dementia:Planning the Road Ahead;staff;http://www.helpguide.org/articles/altheimers-dementia/ dementia-altzheimers-care.htm

Types of Mother-Daughter Relationships: Melody Causewell;http:// e ve r yd a y l i f e . g lo b a lpo st. c om / t y pe s - mot he r- d a u g ht e r- relationships-13135.html

The Structure of the Mother-Daughter Relationship by CareyCross;http://everydaylife.globalpost.com/structure-mother- daughter-relationship-19738.html

Spirituality and Clinical Care by Larry Clifford;British Medical Journal;2002December 21;325(7378):1434-1435;http://www.neb. nlm.nih.gov/pmc/articles/PMC1124896/

Incorporating Religion and Spirituality to Improve care for anxiety and depression in older adults: Laura Phillips, PhD, Amber Paukert PhD, Melinda A. Stanley PhD Mark Chunk, MD, MPH; Journal of Geriatrics;2009;volume64, number8

Types of Dementia: http://altzheimersassociation handbook Stages of Alzheimer's: http://alz.org-handbook.

A Spirituality of Caregiving:Henri.J.M.Noun:Upper Room Books;2011; spirituality series;Henri Noun Society;www.henrinouwen.org

A Tapestry of Love:The Spirituality of Caregiving; Daphne eRiley and Joseph LaGuardia; 2013 2nd edition; www.AtapestryofLove.com

Aging, Spirituality, and Religion: A Handbook:Melvin Kimble, Susan

H. McFadden, PhD;Fortress Press; volume 2(2003) alz.org;Treatments for Behavior:Bulletin, article/newsletter Alzheimer's Association; alz.org;What is Dementia

Mayo Clinic Neurology Research Division; Alzheimer's and related Dementia

Senior Living Blog; Top 7 Physical Alzheimer's symptoms; http://www.aplaceformom.com/blog/alzheimers-physical-changes-7-9-13/.

http://Senior Connection/Alternative treatments/article/alzheimers-dementia/alz.com/; 2015.

Paula Spencer Scott;2009;http://www.caring.com/ blogs/caring-currents/forgetting-faces-what-i... campaign=alz:early_severe_memory1&cu

How not to Take it seriously by Paula Spencer Scott; http://www.caring. com2011/blogs/self-caring

http://www.helpguide.org/home-pages/alzheimers-dementia.htm.

http://www.helpguide.org/articles/alzheimers-dementia/alzheimers-dementia-prevention.htm.

http://www.helpguide.org/Harvard/whats-causing-your-memory-loss.htm

http://www.aplaceformom.com/blog/communication-with-a-loved-one-with-dementia.htm

http://www.aplaceformom.com/blog/2013-02-08-dealing-with-dementia-behavior.htm

Ingram Content Group UK Ltd.
Milton Keynes UK
UKHW010624060423
419743UK00001B/40